THE EXCEPTIONALS

Bob Clyman

BROADWAY PLAY PUBLISHING INC
New York
www.broadwayplaypublishing.com
info@broadwayplaypublishing.com

Cover art by Doug Katz, JamArtz.com
First printing: October 2014
I S B N: 978-0-88145-606-6
Book design: Marie Donovan
Page make-up: Adobe Indesign
Typeface: Palatino

THE EXCEPTIONALS was developed at the Ashland Playwrights New Play Festival and received its world premiere at the Merrimack Repertory Theatre in Lowell, Massachusetts, on 13 February 2011. The cast and creative contributors were:

CLAIRE .... Judith Lightfoot Clarke
GWEN .... Carolyn Baeumler
ALLIE .... Catherine Eaton
TOM .... Joseph Tisa

Director .... Charles Towers
Set .... Judy Gailen
Lighting .... Brian Lilienthal
Costumes .... Deb Newhall
Sound .... Jason Weber
Stage manger .... Emily McMullen

THE EXCEPTIONALS was subsequently produced by The Contemporary American Theater Festival in Shepherdstown, West Virginia, and opened on 6 July 2012. The cast and creative contributors were:

CLAIRE .... Deirdre Madigan
GWEN .... Rebecca Harris
ALLIE .... Anne Marie Nest
TOM .... Joseph Tisa

Director .... Tracy Brigden
Set .... Luciana Stecconi
Lighting .... John Ambrosone
Costumes .... Trevor Bowen
Sound .... James Whoolery
Stage manager .... Lori Doyle

CHARACTERS & SETTING

GWEN, *30s; a mother; quick, brittle, anxious and high-strung*

ALLIE, *30s; a mother; feisty, irreverent, subversive*

TOM, *30s;* ALLIE'*s husband; gregarious, seemingly confident but sensitive to slights*

CLAIRE, *40s; extremely bright, enigmatic, strategic*

Setting: The site of a donor insemination research program for "exceptional" children and their parents. The scenes take place in either the Director of Parent Services' office or the adjacent waiting room. There are two chairs, a love seat and a coffee table in the waiting room. In the office, a desk, a chair, and a mirror along one wall.

Time: The foreseeable future

NOTE

The use of back slash (/) marks towards the end of a line signifies where the next character speaking should interrupt.

If a back slash precedes an ellipsis (/…) at the end of a line, the interruption should come in as quickly as possible after the last word but not interrupt it.

If a line ends with an ellipsis but no back slash, the lack of a full stop usually suggests that the character was about to say more but then changed his/her mind.

If an ellipsis takes place within a speech rather than at the end of it, it usually means the character has interrupted himself to pursue a different thought.

If I think the director and actor might have trouble guessing what the character would have said if she/he had continued, I include those words with parentheses around them before the ellipsis.

ACT ONE

(A light comes up on CLAIRE, *downstage. She addresses an audience.)*

CLAIRE: So imagine someone just created an exceptional new kind of rose. They're only available at a special place, and you can only take home a few at a time. But when you plant them, they transform your garden completely. "There couldn't possibly be a more beautiful garden", you think, but soon you're back to get a few more, and then a few more, and each time your garden is that much more beautiful. Everyone you know drops by to marvel. They ask if it's all right to take a few cuttings, and of course you let them, because there can never be too much beauty in the world. Even the bees are smitten by these roses. They hover for hours, longing for a chance to pollinate them. Sunlight seems to linger just a bit longer on them at the end of the day. And there don't seem to be as many weeds now. It's as if they've receded to make way for this glorious profusion of fragrance, color and beauty. *(Slight beat)* I like to talk about roses, because even the word conjures up visions of a better, more exceptional world. What about the word "exceptional" …is there really such a thing? Some people will tell you there isn't…that everything's a matter of taste, but I think those people aren't being honest. We all know "exceptional" when we see it…and once we have, we can never really be happy with anything less.

(As lights go down on CLAIRE, *a concentrated light comes up on* GWEN, *mid-thirties and conservatively dressed. She is sitting tensely and appears to be waiting. After several beats, more general lighting reveals she is in a waiting room.* ALLIE, *mid-thirties and more casually attired, has just entered and is standing near the door, purse slung over her shoulder and a Dunkin Donuts styrofoam cup.)*

ALLIE: *(After holding a couple of beats)* Hi. You waiting to see Margo?

GWEN: Yes.

ALLIE: Me too. That new assistant what's her name said for me and my husband to be here at ten.

GWEN: You must have heard her wrong…*my* appointment's for ten.

ALLIE: *(Slight beat)* You just checking out places, or have you used them before?

GWEN: We picked the donor for our son here. Ethan.

ALLIE: Great name. How old is he?

GWEN: Five.

ALLIE: Really? Same with Michael. He your only so far?

GWEN: Yes.

ALLIE: Tom and I are thinking about a second, but there are some issues. *(As she takes a crumpled piece of paper from her purse)* Is your husband coming?

GWEN: Ex-husband.

ALLIE: Oh, I'm…

GWEN: It's fine. Trust me.

*(*ALLIE *smoothes out the page before handing it to* GWEN*)*

GWEN: Which one of these do you like best in case it's a girl?

GWEN: Isn't that something you and your husband / should...

ALLIE: How about Sarah?

GWEN: Sure.

ALLIE: Tom refuses to talk about names. He's afraid of getting too attached in case something happens. He started freaking out with Michael the moment we put a deposit down on the sperm. I said to him, "Tom, you can't be attached already, the donor's barely had time to zip up his pants".

GWEN: *(Smiling weakly)* Huh.

ALLIE: He thinks I can't understand, because I didn't have a brother that was only two when he drowned.

GWEN: I can't even imagine what that would be like.

ALLIE: It wasn't like *anything*...Tom wasn't even born yet! How can a fully grown man still be grieving over something he never went through in the first place, it doesn't make sense?!

GWEN: Obviously you know the circumstances / a great (deal better)...

ALLIE: *(A sudden fondness)* Although I don't know... there's actually something very..."Tom" about it. *(Slight beat)* He should be here any second...he just had a really important job interview.

(ALLIE knocks on wood. GWEN smiles, then reaches into her purse, takes out a professional journal and flips to a particular article.)

ALLIE: Looks technical...is that for work?

GWEN: *(Barely acknowledging the question)* Umm.

ALLIE: Are you a scientist?

GWEN: Yes.

ALLIE: What's it about?

GWEN: Like you were saying…it's technical.

(GWEN *Turns back to the article, as* ALLIE *stares at her*)

ALLIE: Are you in Platinum?

GWEN: *(Slight beat)* Why?

ALLIE: You are, aren't you? Margo said only the top two percent of the moms here get picked / for Platinum.

GWEN: If I *were* in Platinum, I don't think Margo would want me to discuss it. The mothers in Platinum are part of an important study.

ALLIE: I don't mind telling you which group I'm in.

GWEN: Do you know anything about research? In a well designed study, no one in the study is supposed to discuss it. Just saying you're <u>in</u> the study could skew the results.

ALLIE: Boy, some of those tests were *hard*.

GWEN: Did you understand what I / just said?

ALLIE: How the fuck do <u>I</u> know what 'shallow brooks are noisy' means?

GWEN: I don't know how to be any / clearer.

ALLIE: Although I think I aced that one with all the inkblots that look like penises?

GWEN: Would you / please stop…?

ALLIE: I'm teasing you.

GWEN: Why?

ALLIE: I know we just met, but you remind me of Mount Vesuvius a couple of seconds before it blew. I'm only trying to help.

GWEN: By teasing me?

ALLIE: That's what I do with Tom whenever *he* gets tense.

GWEN: Has it ever worked? *(Slight beat)* I just think when you're in a waiting room, and somebody asks you nicely, / (the least)...

ALLIE: Hold that thought. *(Reaching for her cell phone, she reads the message with obvious displeasure)*

GWEN: Your husband?

ALLIE: Yeah, you want me to read it to you?

GWEN: I don't think he'd / appreciate...

ALLIE: "Traffic on the Thruway." Like name me a time since the Middle Ages there wasn't.

GWEN: *(Slight beat, then indicating her journal)* I should probably get back / to my...

ALLIE: No problem...I have a book. I never go anywhere without a book.

(ALLIE reaches into her purse and pulls out a paperback with a bright pink cover. GWEN stares at it in disbelief, then resumes reading.)

ALLIE: I just finished *Rogue* by Danielle Steele. The plot was okay, but the sex stuff was nowhere near as...you know the one I mean...by Cassie Edwards?

GWEN: Uh-huh.

ALLIE: Isn't she terrific?

GWEN: I've never even heard of Cassie, whatever you said her / name was.

ALLIE: I'll bet you read a lot to Ethan.

GWEN: I try to.

ALLIE: Michael's subject is math.

GWEN: *(Trying to get back to her work)* Really?

ALLIE: He probably gets that from me.

GWEN: Uh-huh.

ALLIE: It takes me two seconds max to work out the tip in a restaurant.

GWEN: Huh.

ALLIE: *(Beat)* So what do you leave, fifteen, eighteen… as a tip?

GWEN: It depends…I don't / know.

ALLIE: Twenty, if the service was really great?

GWEN: I guess.

ALLIE: Make up some amount your dinner just cost. I'll tell you for fifteen, eighteen, figure the tax / is…

GWEN: What is your / point?

ALLIE: Since you're asking, I really don't like being patronized.

GWEN: How was I patronizing you?

ALLIE: *(Pointing at GWEN's journal)* "It's technical"? *(Slight beat)* I'll bet you'd be pretty upset if I was in Platinum too.

GWEN: Why would I care what group / you're in?

ALLIE: I mean, if *I'm* in the top two per cent, the standards / must not…

GWEN: I don't believe in judging / people *(based on)*…

ALLIE: Well, I / *am.*

GWEN: You are not. *(Beat, then suddenly flaring)* Why isn't that assistant at her desk?! This could never have happened when *Olive* was here. If you and I had shown up at the same time, Olive would have asked one of us to wait in the atrium. No…Olive ran a tight ship. She would have never created this kind of chaos and then abandoned her post.

ALLIE: *(Slight beat)* Have you ever run into another mom in the waiting room like this?

GWEN: No.

ALLIE: In the parking lot?

GWEN: You're the first mom I've seen since I joined the program.

ALLIE: I don't think it's a mistake. Did you get a certified letter saying to be here at ten and plan on staying all day?

GWEN: Don't worry, Margo's going to walk in here and get this whole thing straightened out. *(Looking at her watch, uncertainly)* I mean, they can't just kick us out... this is a *longitudinal* study. They have five years of data on Ethan. As long as our daily logs are in by the end of month... *(Slight beat. Then, with difficulty)* I'm sorry if I...*sounded* like I was patronizing you.

ALLIE: We're good. *(Slight beat)* Must be cool being a scientist. I could never sit still that long. What've you got, a Ph.D?

GWEN: Yes. Well, except for my orals.

ALLIE: What happened?

GWEN: You know...life.

ALLIE: Gotcha.

GWEN: Not that I've ever let it stop me. There's a lot you can do with a Master's Degree in molecular biology. Like teach.

ALLIE: What do you teach?

GWEN: *(Slight beat)* Earth science.

ALLIE: *(Sensing GWEN's embarrassment)* Truthfully, I have no idea how I made it into the study.

GWEN: Well, picture the way a bell curve slopes down approaching a line in both directions. For every person all the way on the right, there's got to be another person all the way…I mean in general, not you / in particular…

ALLIE: You mean the asymptote. *(Slight beat)* The line those slopey things approach at either end? Some people say "a…*symp*…tote", but I never pronounce the "p".

GWEN: I always pronounce the "p".

ALLIE: It's a free country. *(Slight beat)* Margo's always ragging at me to go back to school, because according to the scan they did, my genes have a ton of potential, even though I hide it pretty good.

GWEN: You should definitely take her up…the program will pay your tuition.

ALLIE: Half the classes are after Tom gets home, and I'm busy making dinner.

GWEN: That's just an excuse. Margo's right…someone in Platinum who can't be bothered to finish college… there's a word for that.

ALLIE: Incongruous?

GWEN: *(Surprised and unsettled by* ALLIE's *vocabulary)* No…waste.

ALLIE: You ever have shit like that come out of your mouth, you've got no idea where it came from?

GWEN: I had a student once…your exact situation, and I told her , "The / best…"

ALLIE: Shit! Did I remember to knock on wood right after I mentioned his job interview?

GWEN: I think so.

ALLIE: Thank God. You're Catholic, right?

GWEN: What makes you think that?

ALLIE: Call it a hunch. I'm basically an atheist, but I believe there's a force in the universe that unless you remember to knock on wood, you're totally fucked. *(Beat)* Truthfully, I only joined this study because of all the things they cover we could've never afforded for Michael. Just the medical benefits, but then getting to send Michael to Hill Crest, this school that costs maybe twenty, thirty grand, and that's just tuition… *(Finding it harder to conceal her anxiety)* …I mean the amount it costs to buy your kid a frigging soccer uniform these days…and now with Tom out of work…they can't kick Michael out, just because I flipped Margo a little attitude…she was saying how the Platinum donors here have to agree to get a vasectomy after twenty-four kids.

GWEN: There's a perfectly sound mathematical reason.

ALLIE: I told her it sounded like something a psychotic child dictator would make people do.

GWEN: Anything higher than twenty-four creates an unacceptable risk that two children from the same donor might accidentally meet.

ALLIE: And?

GWEN: Well, if one was a boy and the other a girl, they would be brother and sister.

(Slight beat, as ALLIE waits for her to continue)

GWEN: Right?

ALLIE: Still with you.

GWEN: So…let's say they happen to meet at a party. They've each had a little too much to drink…do I really need to explain this to you?

ALLIE: So they have sex? It took a lot more than one brother and sister to create Mississippi.

GWEN: Even if *they're* perfectly normal, the odds of a defective baby, because each of them has a copy of the same rare *(gene)*…and the screening here, compared to other programs…why are you making me prove it's better *not* to have incest? Even men who clearly tested Platinum were weeded out if the scan found another defective / gene…

ALLIE: I think it's the 'weeding out' part that makes me uneasy.

GWEN: Ninety-eight percent of the mothers here can't get into Platinum, so their child won't be like Ethan or Michael…how is that any different?

ALLIE: That's the problem, it isn't. Tell me you don't have *any* qualms about this whole "Uber- sperm" Platinum thing.

GWEN: Did somebody put a gun to your head and make you join the program? This is the first serious attempt to study exceptional, donor-inseminated children, and personally I feel grateful that Ethan and I have the privilege / of playing a part.

ALLIE: *(Ignoring* GWEN'*s speech,* ALLIE *has started to read a text when she bursts out laughing)* Just something Janice… *(She reads on, bursts out laughing even harder this time, then puts her phone back.)*

GWEN: *(A couple of beats)* I was just wondering…since we both have appointments at ten, would you mind letting me go first?

ALLIE: Kind of.

GWEN: I'm just a little nervous, that's all.

ALLIE: They're not gonna kick *Ethan* out of the program. If anyone should be nervous, / I'm…

GWEN: Your husband isn't even here yet.

ALLIE: So I'll start without him.

GWEN: It's always better to start together when you're a couple.

ALLIE: They have research on that?

GWEN: Who knows when he'll even get here?

ALLIE: He's probably less than / five minutes…

GWEN: *(About to lose it)* Fine, if you really need me to say it…please?

ALLIE: *(Beat)* Okay.

GWEN: Thank you. *(She resumes reading her article)* Now was that so hard?

(Before ALLIE can respond, the office door opens. ALLIE and GWEN are clearly surprised to see someone other than Margo enter the room.)

CLAIRE: Hi, my name is Dr. Lindstrom, please call me Claire. *I'll* be meeting with you today.

GWEN: What happened to Margo?

CLAIRE: She won't be in.

GWEN: Is everything all right?

CLAIRE: *(Slight beat, as she looks at GWEN with a mixture of curiosity and surprise)* Of course. I was expecting a Tom?

ALLIE: He's stuck in traffic.

CLAIRE: *(Gesturing towards her office)* Shall we?

GWEN: You want to see us together?

CLAIRE: (ALLIE *starts to follow. Ignoring* GWEN's *question,* CLAIRE *points to* ALLIE's *empty, styrofoam coffee cup)* Did you want to leave that?

(As GWEN follows CLAIRE into the office, ALLIE goes back for the cup. Unable to find a wastebasket, she takes it with her, but unable to find one there either, she puts it near her on the desk.)

CLAIRE: How's Ethan feeling…I understand he's out today?

GWEN: A little cold…my sister's watching him. His school called you about a cold?

(CLAIRE *has begun to focus on one of the two large files on her desk.*)

GWEN: Is that all Ethan?

CLAIRE: *(Flipping through pages)* I guess it beats paying a fourteen-year-old to talk on the phone.

GWEN: What does?

CLAIRE: Having your sister watch him. *(Her eyes lingering on something)* Things a little better between you?

GWEN: Why, what does it (say)…I don't remember telling Margo… *(As much to* ALLIE*)* We're just very different, that's all.

CLAIRE: Takes more after your mom?

(Slight beat. GWEN *is becoming more rattled, due as much to* CLAIRE*'s suden shift as the questions themselves.)*

CLAIRE: Considering how close you were with your dad. *(Quickly glancing at* ALLIE*)* You don't mind, do you? *(Without waiting for* ALLIE *to respond)* At least it was quick. *(Slight beat)* Aneurysm, right?

GWEN: Yes.

CLAIRE: No surprise he collected model trains. *(Slight beat)* Your father. *(Slight beat)* Since Ethan does.

GWEN: Oh, I (see)…yes.

CLAIRE: *(Beat, then to* ALLIE, *without even a glance this time)* Anything *you* need to say, or can we start?

ALLIE: I'm good.

CLAIRE: *(To both of them)* A few months ago the team completed its first major analysis of the data.

GWEN: Really?

CLAIRE: Nothing we didn't expect, but... *(To* GWEN*)* ...you've done enough research yourself, Gwen...I'm sure you remember how excited...when your data didn't merely confirm...they *exceeded*...

GWEN: I certainly do.

CLAIRE: *(Including* ALLIE*)* Remember, these are only trends, not definitive / results.

GWEN: No, I understand.

CLAIRE: As with any longitudinal / study...

GWEN: That's exactly what I was telling her.

CLAIRE: *(Beat, as she gives* GWEN *a cautioning look)* Five years ago, the team began to develop a new model, based on the research, for unlocking the full potential of a child's mind. With each new discovery, the team refined the model a little more, until it became so precise we were able to create an actual school. I've spent these past five years preparing for the day we'd be ready to start taking students...and now we are. *(Slight beat)* A lot of people will be paying close attention and judging us, so we've had to be particularly selective in choosing our first group of children, and...with so many outstanding children to choose from, and since we'll only be taking twelve, unfortunately...we were only able to include the most exceptional in our current group of finalists, which... *fortunately* includes Ethan *and* Michael, so whatever happens next, they each deserve a round of applause for getting this far.

GWEN: *(Slight beat)* I'm speechless.

CLAIRE: Before we can make our final / decisions...

GWEN: Is that why I'm here?

CLAIRE: Why you're *both* here.

GWEN: I'm not in trouble?

CLAIRE: No. Should you be?

GWEN: No.

(Slight, awkward beat)

ALLIE: I'm fine with the school Michael's in now.

CLAIRE: It's an excellent school, but even...what's that name they have for the track he's in?

ALLIE: Triple G. *(To GWEN)* They have three tracks at Michael's school.

CLAIRE: If a child tests smarter than a loaf of zucchini bread, he's automatically in the "gifted" track. Then there's the "gifted, gifted" track if he's average...

ALLIE: The kids in Triple G are smart.

CLAIRE: But still a couple of "Gs" short of Michael.

GWEN: *(Less to inform than to keep the focus as much on Ethan)* It's the exact same thing with Ethan at Bryce.

ALLIE: Where I went to school, they only had *two* tracks..."normal" and "retarded"...worked for me. Look, I know the work isn't always as challenging, but Ms Edie tries...there's a whole shelf of books just for Michael, and he's finally starting to make friends.

CLAIRE: Friends like that are fine, but he needs peers, and they aren't peers.

ALLIE: *(Slight beat)* I know.

GWEN: Same with Ethan...nice school but no peers.

CLAIRE: *(Handing GWEN and ALLIE several typed pages)* This is only an overview. Doctor Vorsiff will explain everything after lunch.

GWEN: Doctor Vorsiff wants to meet with *us*?

CLAIRE: I'd be misleading you if I didn't say a number of slots are already filled.

GWEN: Oh. Well, as long as Ethan...how many?

CLAIRE: A few of those children, you might as well throw out your computer and replace it with them, but we need the right blend. It's like an orchestra. Even if the best musicians in town all played the cello, you wouldn't want to hear Beethoven's 9th played / only by...

GWEN: I know what a *blend* is. *(Concerned her response may have been too aggressive)* So if Ethan isn't a cello, what is he?

CLAIRE: A flute.

GWEN: Why a flute?

CLAIRE: Why is Michael another flute? Why is Emma Harris a clarinet? *(She appears to be considering the questions and how how to best answer it but then turns to* ALLIE *instead.)* Any news on Tom?

ALLIE: I'm not even getting a signal.

CLAIRE: I need some time alone with Gwen anyway. Would you mind waiting out there?

(As ALLIE *starts to exit,* CLAIRE *stares at her coffee cup, which* ALLIE *has forgotten. As if giving her a chance to remember,* CLAIRE *waits until she is almost out the door.)*

CLAIRE: And taking that cup with you?

*(*ALLIE *turns back, looks at the cup, then up at* CLAIRE*)*

CLAIRE: Thank you.

*(*ALLIE *hesitates before getting it. She then walks through the waiting room to wait outside for* TOM.*)*

GWEN: So when you're choosing...I assume you also take their mothers into account?

CLAIRE: I'm not sure / I (follow)...

GWEN: Children take their lead from us...the sort of books we read...

CLAIRE: Is your / point...?

GWEN: I'm just saying if one parent reads novels by Cassie Steele…

CLAIRE: Who?

GWEN: Cassie Steele.

CLAIRE: I think you may be mixing up Cassie Edwards and Danielle / Steele…

GWEN: All I know is the cover was so pink it nearly blinded me.

CLAIRE: *(She opens* GWEN's *file and flips pages)* Try not to think of this as a competition. I mean, in a way it *is*… in a way that's *exactly* what it is…but… *(Having found what she wanted)* It's Pete, right? Your ex-husband…you call him Pete?

GWEN: Right?

CLAIRE: I was going over the sign in sheets from school, and it looks like *you* dropped Ethan off two Mondays in a row.

GWEN: Pete had to miss a weekend…something with his girlfriend's family in Seattle.

CLAIRE: Doesn't he get to swap?

GWEN: If he asks. You're not saying I should *force* Ethan on him?

CLAIRE: No, but if Pete pulls away, how you will ever find time for yourself?

GWEN: That weekend the train museum had a special exhibit. Ethan loves all those Pullman cars from the twenties…the brass railings and walnut panels…if you could've seen his eyes…how could any mother need more than that?

CLAIRE: I see…still not dating.

GWEN: I really don't see what this / has to do with …?

CLAIRE: On the last questionnaire, you thought you were ready, and that was six months ago.

GWEN: I can't just snap my fingers, I'm not twenty-five.

CLAIRE: No, and at your age you can't afford to waste six months. You're still an attractive woman…have you tried the internet?

GWEN: I'm not looking that kind of thing.

CLAIRE: I don't know what stories you've heard, but there are plenty of discreet services these days for busy, professional women who want a dignified alternative to being fondled in a club. I'm wasting my breath, aren't I?

GWEN: About that.

CLAIRE: *(Beat. She lets the silence build. A sudden shift in energy)* While we're pausing, when you asked about Margo, and I didn't really answer, you may have guessed I didn't want to discuss it in front of Allie, but the truth is we had to let her go.

GWEN: Let her go?

CLAIRE: Don't think it was easy, but she ran Parent Services…she *supervised* Olive …so when we discovered the damage Olive almost caused by ignoring procedures…what choice did we have but to let *both* of them go? *(Slight beat)* It might surprise you, but in all my years, I've never known a single Platinum donor by his actual name. Yours for instance has always been C2 to me as he is to you. Conversely, if C2 ever needed to ask about Ethan, he'd've said "how is C2 hypen 17?" Because the right to privacy for both… which is why we *have* the procedures, right?

GWEN: I'm not really sure which procedures / you're…

CLAIRE: In return for their "donations", if you will, we have allowed these exceptional men the unique opportunity to remain informed about their offspring by sending them monthly reports. No personal details, of course, and Olive's job was to scrub each report for anything that could possibly identify a child...then ask the parent to read it over carefully just to be sure. Once the parent returned it to her, all Olive had to do off was proof it one last time herself before mailing it, but Olive...dear, dear Olive only saw the good in people and trusted them...which is how one of the mothers could take a flash memory card...those things some people use to record their own voice instead of writing a letter...? and slip it between two pages...they're about yay big...? *(She removes a flash memory card from between two pages in Ethan's file and shows it to* GWEN*)* So when C2 opened the last report on Ethan, he would've found this recording from you. *(She goes to the door and opens it.)* Still no Tom? Gwen's going to get herself some soup and come back in an hour.

(As GWEN *starts to speak,* CLAIRE *stops her.)*

CLAIRE: Not until you've had soup. If you go less than a mile on Durant, there's a cute little place called "Grist for the Mill"...their tomato basil is the best.

*(*GWEN *seems frozen but then suddenly exits with a brisk, purposeful stride.* CLAIRE *gestures for* ALLIE *to sit.)*

CLAIRE: So, did you have a chance to look at / those...

ALLIE: Before we get to the school, can I bring something up? *(Slight beat)* Tom and I think it's time for another child.

CLAIRE: Allie, that's wonderful.

ALLIE: Michael's been begging us for over a year.

CLAIRE: The team will be thrilled.

ALLIE: Tom and I would love... *(Knocking on wood)* ...a little girl. My sister Beth took a ton of potassium, or Edie might've been Eddie.

CLAIRE: The new donor catalogue just came in. Do you and Tom want to look today?

ALLIE: Right now his job situation…

CLAIRE: Understood.

ALLIE: *(Knocking on wood again)* …which may be about to change, but until he actually *has* / something…

CLAIRE: If you're worried about the money, we're completely / behind you on…

ALLIE: *(With greater intensity)* I just don't want to cause any problems here for Michael. *(Slight beat)* Please don't take this…Tom adores Michael. He just feels maybe this time we should pick a donor from one of your other groups. Someone who's more, you know… average.

CLAIRE: "Average."

ALLIE: Truthfully, if it was up to Tom, we'd adopt.

CLAIRE: Even though *you're* still perfectly capable / of having…?

ALLIE: And I *want* that, but doesn't it seem kind of selfish when he *can't*. And I agree that adopting… every time I hear some kid got left in a dumpster, but I *still* want my own. *(Slight beat)* When my mom died, all my friends were there for me, but my *sisters* got me through. Even now, just knowing I can call Janet or Beth, I feel safer, so if anything ever happened to me and Tom /…

CLAIRE: You'd want Michael and *his* sister to have what you…no, I / understand.

ALLIE: Janet's dumber than a box of hair, but she's still my sister, so even if our new donor guy's more like Janet /…

CLAIRE: It isn't that simple. The world has changed since you had Michael. Mothers are a lot more particular. Five years ago, you could've found half a dozen Toms in our Silver catalogue, but nowadays… and it isn't just here. Nobody's taking average…there's no demand.

ALLIE: *(Pointing to the file)* You have it in there Tom's dyslexic?

*(*CLAIRE *nods.)*

ALLIE: It didn't get picked up till high school, so he grew up assuming he was retarded. When the lady who did the testing told him he's dyslexic, Tom broke down and cried. He said it wasn't fair having whatever she just called him on top of being retarded.

(A small chuckle from CLAIRE*)*

ALLIE: Cut to twelve years later…Tom just found out he's sterile. So we wind up here, and Tom picks up that brochure on how great you are at keeping anyone with a genetic defect who wants to donate from slipping through. He flips the page to see who you're calling defective, and right near the top is dyslexia.

(Noticing CLAIRE *glance at her watch)*

ALLIE: I know the idea when we started here was if we ever decide to have more kids…as long as Michael is still in the program…do you understand what I'm asking?

CLAIRE: I *think* you're asking will Michael be terminated from the program, if you refuse a platinum donor this time.

ALLIE: Will he? *(Indicating* CLAIRE's *watch)* I know we're supposed to be talking about the new school, but if you're just gonna toss Michael out, / (there's no point)…

CLAIRE: I'm still not clear. I can see why *Tom* wants a donor who's average like him, but is that / what *you* /...?

ALLIE: Not like *him*. Like *us*. I know I test like a major geek, but those scores aren't *me*.

CLAIRE: Granted you're a little rough around the edges, but forget the scores...your genetic scan was one of the most exceptional / out of...

ALLIE: If I have all this potential laying dormant, shouldn't *some* of it be awake by now?

CLAIRE: "Lying" dormant.

ALLIE: There, you see.

CLAIRE: What I see is someone who knows "lying dormant" is right but chooses to say it wrong. *(Slight beat)* Personally I think Tom deserves a world of credit. Some husbands, just the *idea* of a donor...

ALLIE: So if it means that much to him...?

CLAIRE: I understand, but what about *you*...as Michael's *mother*? Don't you think a little sister who's more like Michael / would offer...

ALLIE: That's what I said to Tom, but he feels *very* / strongly...

CLAIRE: I know what *Tom* feels, it's all I keep hearing... what I *don't* understand... *(Slight beat)* I realize you only joined this study for..."practical" reasons. You're different from the other moms. They all take their children to foreign films and tell them fruit is a dessert. You have a rebel streak, and personally, I find that appealing, but you and I aren't booking a cruise, and if you're telling me you'd be willing to deprive your second child of the same advantages Michael...just so she can match up better with Tom / ...?

ALLIE: *(Sharply)* You have no idea what it's like for Tom. He has so much love to give, but when he's with Michael…he feels smaller. So if he's just gonna wind up feeling he doesn't measure up again…

CLAIRE: Michael does that to people. Did his teacher tell you the problem he's having in groups?

ALLIE: That's not his / (fault) …?

CLAIRE: I'm not saying it / is.

ALLIE: Ms. Edie loves breaking the class into small groups and letting them compete to see which group can figure some problem out first. And I get how that *could* be fun, except the kids in Michael's group just sit with their thumbs up their butts while Michael solves it, and the kids in every other group know they're going to lose, so they give up and start screwing around, which really pisses Ms. Edie off. She's always saying, "I can't blame Michael for being so smart", but I know she does.

CLAIRE: It won't take him long to figure out if he just pretends to get a few answers wrong…

ALLIE: He already has.

CLAIRE: I wonder who he gets *that* from? *(Beat)* Do you really want to make him go through the same thing you did in school?

ALLIE: *(Slight beat)* What am I supposed to do with that? You think it doesn't kill me to see him pretend he's interested like I did when he's bored out of his frigging mind? If anyone should know how to help him…but I don't have a fucking clue. No one's invited him over to play in months, and this is *with* the program. What's gonna happen to him if you kick him out?

CLAIRE: I'm not saying we will. It's not like there's a policy…we haven't needed one. You're the first

parents to ask us for a second baby who isn't as smart
as the first. What I *do* know is by the time we decide,
every slot for the school will be full, so I guess I'm
saying…and believe me, I really don't mean this as a
threat…although I suppose you could take it as one…
Michael could end up with nothing.

(After a beat, TOM *enters.)*

TOM: Sorry, you wouldn't believe the traffic… *(He
notices* CLAIRE*)*

CLAIRE: You must be Tom. I'm Doctor Lindstrom…
Claire.

TOM: What happened, did Margo get canned?

CLAIRE: Unfortunately, I'm not at liberty / to…

TOM: Hey, nothing's forever…especially now with the
whole world going global. *(He drops a bag with some
donuts on her desk and begins putting them onto paper
plates. While his manner suggests a good-natured, expansive
salesman, the pressure of his speech suggest hints at some
underlying anxiety.)* Does Bavarian Creme work for
you? Margo *loved* / Bavarian…

ALLIE: You stopped for donuts?

TOM: *Before* my interview…is that okay?

CLAIRE: Since we're starting a little late…

TOM: I know, you think they could shut down *one*
lane on the Thruway instead of two, since no one's
ever working on either. Maybe *you* can tell me. Has
anyone ever found a gene for religion? Right before
my interview, I was flipping through a magazine,
and it turns out a light goes on in somebody's brain
when he's feeling connected to God, which I've never
personally…so if it only happens to *some* people, what if
there's a gene / that…

CLAIRE: There isn't.

TOM: Sorry…way too much coffee.

CLAIRE: But it's an interesting thought.

TOM: It's yours…I've got a dozen more just like it. Some guy told me he tries to come up with one new idea whenever he's stuck in traffic. He learned that in anger management.

(Noticing ALLIE's *expression)*

TOM: What?

ALLIE: The interview?

TOM: *(To* CLAIRE*)* How much do you know about calibration devices?

(As TOM *expected,* CLAIRE *indicates "not very much".)*

TOM: Let's say you bought a piece of electrical equipment two years ago, and lately… *(Quickly to* ALLIE*)* …this'll just take a minute… *(Back to* CLAIRE*)* …the readings seem a little off. A good calibration device tells you by how much, so you can adjust, but what if your calibration device is off too? I've seen low end devices that were even less accurate than the equipment they were trying to calibrate.

CLAIRE: Interesting.

TOM: Yeah, well you try doing it fifteen years. So it was either keep doing it another fifteen and hope I can save enough to retire early like Joe / is doing…

ALLIE: His old boss.

TOM: …or be proactive and do something *now.*

CLAIRE: So leaving was *your* decision?

TOM: Well, not exactly…I was let go, but Joe's a pretty astute reader of men, and he said my non-verbals were coming through loud and clear. Of course it doesn't take long to start missing the paycheck, so when this headhunter called about Murphy and Finn…better product line, big hike in pay…of course I've done my homework, I know exactly what this guy needs, so I start right in, and he's loving it. I'm only penciled in for thirty minutes, but it's been fifty, and I'm still on a roll, when halfway through a sentence I stop, because it's suddenly clear…so I tell him, "Look, Murph"…that's what he asked me to call him…"Murph"… "I could do this job in my sleep and *still* make you money, but hearing myself aloud, I know that coming on board at this juncture would be a colossal mistake. If I don't take stock of my life and figure out what I really want, I probably never will." So Murph leans back and starts telling me how after his wife divorced him, he drank a fifth of scotch a day, ignored his person hygiene and started keeping a loaded gun in his desk, until his sponsor made him take a personal inventory, which looking back was the single most important thing he ever did. *(Beat. Disconcerted by the lack of reaction, he is at a loss but then throws himself into his other argument.)* And *truthfully*, I'm not terribly sanguine about where the calibration industry is heading in this country. Don't be surprised if you wake up one morning, and the entire *concept* has been shipped overseas. But if you want to think "big picture" …for every guy who's standing there with a pink slip saying life isn't fair… that's maybe four guys in Mexico who finally have a job…you know what I mean?

CLAIRE: I think so. I'm just not clear…*while* you're taking stock…how you plan to pay your bills. Allie hasn't worked since Michael, and now with a *second* child…true, we've been able to help with medical insurance and certain / other…

TOM: Aren't those covered by your grant?

CLAIRE: Yes…

TOM: Then why did you say that like we're asking for a handout?

CLAIRE: That's not what / I...

TOM: We're perfectly capable of paying for our own medical insurance.

ALLIE: How?

TOM: *(Thrown by her question)* What do you...? The same way any family...we just would. *(To* CLAIRE*)* Nobody's destitute here. My cousin installs commercial carpeting, he throws me a little work. I'm helping another guy build a deck... *(Back to* ALLIE*)* ...did you tell her what we want to do different this time?

ALLIE: Claire said it isn't that simple. *All* the donors are... *(Looking to* CLAIRE *for support)*

CLAIRE: It's just the market, Tom.

TOM: Then we'll go somewhere else...like we *agreed*.

ALLIE: She said it's the same everywhere.

TOM: So what are you / saying?

ALLIE: I don't know! Maybe if you'd *been* here on time, / I wouldn't...

TOM: What was I supposed to do, stand up and walk out in / the middle?

ALLIE: No, just have your great epiphany at the beginning instead of waiting fifty / minutes.

TOM: My *what*?

ALLIE: Your great...reve / lation.

TOM: I know what a fucking "epiphany" is. I just don't know whose benefit you're using a word like "epiphany" for! *(To* CLAIRE*)* Believe me, she'll be a lot less chichi during the make up sex tonight.

ALLIE: Do you think Claire finds that funny?

TOM: I just *met* the woman. I haven't a fucking clue what she / finds funny...

ALLIE: I'm still curious how we'll get lettuce once all the farmers in Mexico starts retooling for all the jobs in calibration that / are going to...

CLAIRE: You know these issues always stir up / a lot of...

TOM: *(Still to* ALLIE*)* We had an agreement! *(Beat)* Michael's amazing, but I thought we agreed one amazing kid is hard enough.

ALLIE: Maybe we need to try harder.

TOM: Did I miss when someone decided we're not good enough anymore? *(To* CLAIRE*)* My dad...you gave him a hammer, a few nails and some scrap wood, he could build you a house. You had a question about American history, just ask my dad...and wherever he picked that stuff up, it wasn't reading, because it turns out he was dyslexic like me...and what I *think* you're saying...if my mom came to you and said she wanted a kid like my dad, you'd've told her, "Sorry, we don't make that kind of kid anymore".

ALLIE: I know we agreed at home, and maybe it's the best decision for us. I just don't know if Michael...

TOM: You think he's gonna care the baby isn't a genius? He'll be the older brother...he's the one that's supposed to be smart.

ALLIE: What about when she gets a "C", and her teacher says, "Stop saying you tried. No sister of Michael...?'

TOM: Her teacher can't say that if she's adopted. Some kid who actually *needs* / (a home)...

ALLIE: Why are you bringing up adoption, after all the frigging hours it took us to finally agree...

TOM: Oh, so *now* if we agreed on something at home, it suddenly matters again?

(Before ALLIE *can respond,* GWEN *enters.)*

CLAIRE: I thought I said an hour.

GWEN: I know, and I was halfway to that place with the soup when I suddenly realized…

CLAIRE: And it couldn't wait until after lunch?

TOM: *(To* GWEN*)* We're pretty much done in here anyway.

ALLIE: What do you mean?

TOM: What else is there to talk about?

GWEN: First, you tell us there are only a couple of slots…so of course I'm trying especially hard to make a good impression, but then you blindside me by bringing up…that other thing, and you won't let me explain, so I'm driving, my mind's going over and over, and *she's* in here, probably getting treated with kid gloves, and I don't think that's fair.

CLAIRE: Actually, Gwen, I don't see how I could have been any fairer. I thought bringing it up before lunch, you'd have time to regain your composure and decide what you'd *like* to say instead of just reacting like… well, this.

GWEN: *(Slight beat)* Right. *(To* ALLIE *and* TOM, *as she turns to go)* Sorry for the interruption. *(She looks at her watch)* Why don't we make it an hour and *ten* minutes, so you get all of your time. *(She exits.)*

CLAIRE: *(After a couple of beats)* Try something with me. Imagine…just as an exercise…the two of you never got married…never even met. Allie, why don't you go first? One day you're at a party and a celebrity comes over to you. Naturally, you're nervous, but when you look at your watch, you've been talking for hours.

Everyone else is gone. Even the host is gone. You open
the door to leave, but instead of the street, the two of
you are in a bedroom with a single lit candle, and you
start to make passionate love. Which celebrity did you
imagine?

TOM: What?!

CLAIRE: Obviously, you *are* married, and Allie would
never...what I'm trying to get / at...

TOM: Do you have some uncle that got you this job?!

ALLIE: *(As* TOM *turns to her)* Don't look at me, I / didn't
know...

TOM: What did you tell her about our sex life?

ALLIE: Nothing.

TOM: If you don't like something, you should be telling
me / instead of...

CLAIRE: You're both making this much too
complicated. Allie...can you tell me who it was?

(Slight beat, aware that TOM *is staring at her)*

ALLIE: What if it wasn't someone specific?

CLAIRE: Then pretend it *was* someone specific, and tell
me *him.*

ALLIE: *(Beat)* All right, put down George Clooney.

TOM: I can't believe you just said that.

ALLIE: Why, you never said Angelina Jolie was hot?

TOM: Not like that, / I didn't.

ALLIE: I never asked you to name the sexiest person
you / could (think of)...?

TOM: Right, and I said *you*... *(To* CLAIRE) ...but she said
"no, it has to be a movie star". Meanwhile I'm trying to
drive, there's a fucking blizzard, and she's got this *feral*
/ expression...

ALLIE: It was not / *feral...*

TOM: *(To* ALLIE*)* ...so finally I said, "Angelie Jolie, are you satisfied", just to make you stop.

ALLIE: And I said "George Clooney" just to make *her* stop.

TOM: Except when *I* said it, we were driving home from a movie Angelina Jolie was *in.* I can't help if she was the last face I saw.

ALLIE: Actually, the last face you saw was Brad Pitt, how come you didn't pick...? *(To* CLAIRE*)* Can I change to Brad Pitt?

TOM: So when *I* joke about make-up sex, it isn't funny, but it's okay for *you* / to...?

CLAIRE: Can anyone guess the point of my exercise?! *(Beat)* Every woman needs a man to father her child, but how does she know which man? The one who writes beautiful sonnets to her on her birthday but has blotchy skin? The one who pulled her out of a half-frozen lake once and made soup to keep her warm but showed pictures of her naked to his friends? Whoever she chooses, he will be flawed, which is how it should be. She may even truly love this man, and I say thank God for that. It won't do her any good to mope around waiting for George Clooney to send her flowers, and yet almost every woman who tries this pictures him... *but...*and here's my point...she doesn't want George Clooney. She may *think* she does, but what she really wants is his genes.

TOM: *(After a couple of beats, to* ALLIE*)* Why are you looking like that?

ALLIE: Like what?

TOM: Like anything she just said makes any sense. *(Back to* CLAIRE*)* Do you have a husband, kids, because I don't see any pictures / on ...?

CLAIRE: Try to stay with me, Tom. Allie loves you... she has since the two of your were in high school, and she wanted to have *your* children, but, no one's fault, it wasn't to be, so now her instinct...if it has to be a stranger...is to go after the choicest, most exceptional, Platinum genes, so your daughter / can have...

TOM: She *agreed*!

CLAIRE: To *what*, Tom?! Let me guess. It was a long week, the two of you were relaxing over wine, and something you said made her laugh. She wanted to please you...then another glass of wine...you said "adoption"..."average"...she said "when you put it that way, maybe I've been too this or too that", but the thing is, Tom...that isn't what she needs.

TOM: And you're more qualified than I am to know what she needs?

CLAIRE: Apparently. *You* keep wanting to make it personal. Do you feel betrayed every time she ovulates? Well, the need I'm describing has about as much to do with you / as that.

TOM: *(Turning to* ALLIE*)* That's it. I'm not going to sit here / and...

ALLIE: She's right. *(Beat)* I'm sorry. I never cared what kind of child..."as long as he had all his fingers and toes", remember? But once I found out we could choose, and his life would be better...things would come easier...I couldn't say, "No, I want him to struggle like us"...and neither could you.

TOM: *(Conceding)* I know...

ALLIE: And it's not like the first time we held Michael, I was thinking about his genes. He was special, because he was ours. Just getting to take him home and love him / was...

TOM: I understand all that, / Allie...

ALLIE: Let me say this! *(Slight beat)* He didn't have to *do* anything special for me to love him, but then he started to, and I'm sorry…I never thought I could love him even more because of that, but I did. I do. Sometimes I'll just sit there watching him play, and I feel…like I've been invited into this special room where nobody else can go.

CLAIRE: *(Slight beat)* Tom, if Michael could choose the kind of sister…?

TOM: Michael's *five*. The only thing he should be choosing is the kind of ice cream / he…

CLAIRE: I'm just asking if he *could* choose, / what…?

TOM: I don't care! *(To* ALLIE*)* All I keep hearing is what *you* want…what *Michael*…how come nobody's asking me what I want? Why is everyone acting like there's something wrong with wanting a kid who's a little like *me*? *(Slight beat)* A couple of months ago I was asking Michael why he never plays with some toy I bought him. First thing he does is take me to this website about a group that's trying to have the toy recalled because of some tiny magnet a two-year-old choked on and died. Then he showed me how to recognize all the lead from how the light hits the paint, and I'm thinking, "Jesus, it's a fucking toy"…but he was right, and it's not like he was all prissy…the hardest part was how patient… *(Slight beat)* Another time he asked me for help with his homework. I couldn't believe he was already learning to multiply fractions. I said, "Lucky for you, your old man still has a *few* things in his tool kit", and showed him a nifty little shortcut…it felt great. Then I found out the homework was from months ago…he was actually learning quadratic equations…he just asked me to be nice.

ALLIE: Tom, he's the same with / me.

TOM: I'm his father, it's *not* the same! I worshipped my dad, but now *I'm* the dad, and I love Michael, I really do, but I hate this feeling…like he got gypped ending up with me.

CLAIRE: Tom…I know this isn't easy. There's a lot to figure out…the kind of family you want…whether to turn down that job you / interviewed…

TOM: I already did.

CLAIRE: And I heard that, but to turn down a job with benefits when you have a wife…a *child*…a *second* child…no leads…no irons in the fire…nothing one might be tempted to call an actual *plan*…

TOM: *(Furious, he stands)* You think I'm nothing, don't you?

CLAIRE: No, Tom. The only reason I can say these things is I have more faith in you than you do.

(TOM stares at her, throws a glance at ALLIE, then exits. ALLIE starts to go after him.)

CLAIRE: Let him go. Wait half an hour, *then* call him.

ALLIE: This isn't a game.

CLAIRE: No, and he's not a baby, stop trying to protect him. *(Pointing to the pages she gave ALLIE earlier)* I know you're upset, but Doctor Vorsiff needs to meet with you today. When you speak to Tom, ask him to be here by one.

ALLIE: There's no point even *mentioning* the school after / what *(just happened)*…

CLAIRE: Just get him here…Doctor Vorsiff will handle the rest. He has a wonderful way with the fathers, and once he explains / why…

ALLIE: I don't care how "wonderful", Tom's not going to agree just / because…

CLAIRE: Technically speaking, I'm not sure he has to. Your signature should be enough.

ALLIE: *(Beat)* If you're suggesting...Tom's my husband...I would never / do *(anything)*...

CLAIRE: Oh, for Chrissake...he's an *adult*. Michael's an exceptional child, but he's still a child, and he needs a mother, so start acting like one. Instead of obsessing about Tom, why don't you think about the word *mother* and decide what it means to you.

END OF ACT ONE

ACT TWO

(CLAIRE's *office. she now has a shoebox on her desk.* ALLIE *faces her, looking ready for battle.*)

CLAIRE: I told Gwen I'd meet with *her* / right after...

ALLIE: What *is* it with Gwen? When I bumped into her at that soup place, she said she was deciding whether to jump off a bridge. Then she said, "Not *literally*," and started begging me to promise not to tell you, but before I could say "fine", she said, "Oh, do whatever you want, that's what you always do anyway" ...so you know what I think? Fuck *her*. (*Couple of beats, as she tries with diminishing success to maintain this tone of feisty bravado*) That thing you were saying...how I don't need Tom's signature? He and I were watching this show about some lesbian couple with a kid, where the mom who gave birth got custody, and the one who mostly took care of the kid didn't even get visits. I could tell from Tom's expression he was already comparing *our*...so I said, "Maybe the judge has a prejudice against lesbians"...which didn't make any sense since they were *both* lesbians...but then Tom said, "You think *she's* got it bad, when it comes to family court, you've got worse odds being a man than a lesbian," referring to a guy he knows who came home to find his twelve year-old son watching porn on T V, with his wife passed out drunk on the couch right next to him, so he grabbed a camera, took pictures to show the judge, and his wife *still* got the kid, so maybe Tom's right. If someone can lose his kid, because he's only "the father", what about guys like Tom who didn't even kick in the sperm? *(Slight beat)* That's what you meant, isn't it?

CLAIRE: Only if the two of you still can't agree after you've tried to work it out.

ALLIE: *(In a neutral tone, as if simply seeking to clarify a detail)* Did you mean just the school, or I could decide on the donor too?

CLAIRE: I suppose I meant both.

ALLIE: *(Beat)* Michael wet himself. It was last week, right after his teacher told me the problem with groups. I don't think he heard us talking, but while I was tucking him into bed that night, his lip started trembling, and he asked me why Ms Edie doesn't like him anymore. This was over a week ago, and I still haven't told Tom. I just handled it on my own, which is exactly what *you're* suggesting, and I know it's the same as lying, but I can already guess what he'll say. "This is *our* fault...we should've sent him to public school...if those people think we're gonna let them screw up our second kid, too" ...and while he's going through the litany, inside my head I'll be screaming, "Jesus, Tom, I'm his mother! He's what I do all day! How about instead of the drama, you go for a smoke and leave these fucking things to me!"

(GWEN enters.)

GWEN: Perfect.

ALLIE: I'm just cashing in my chit for when I let you go first.

GWEN: Your husband wasn't here.

ALLIE: He could have *gotten* here before Claire / was ready...

GWEN: He could've missed his exit and wound up in China, what's / your point?

ALLIE: My point is I agreed to let you go first, *before* I knew he'd be late / so...

GWEN: Yes, but that was only *after* you gave me an incredibly hard time, even though I asked you nicely, so don't act like you deserve full credit.

ALLIE: *(As she is leaving)* You seriously need to get laid.

(GWEN turns to CLAIRE in disbelief, as ALLIE continues through the waiting room towards the exit.)

CLAIRE: So what's this about wanting to jump off a bridge?

GWEN: *(Beat)* I'll be right back. *(Catching ALLIE before she leaves)* Why did you tell her I wanted to jump off a bridge?

ALLIE: That's what you / said.

GWEN: I know why you're doing this.

ALLIE: Tell me.

GWEN: Spite. You don't even *want* Michael to go. All those snide remarks about the program...you resent me, because I have something I really believe in.

ALLIE: You think I'd decide Michael's future based on how I'm less than nuts about *you*?

GWEN: Well, no...I guess I don't really (believe that) ...Can't you see how unfair ...?! I'm completely committed to the program, and if Ethan could get in...

ALLIE: Are you asking me to keep Michael where he is, just so Ethan can go?

GWEN: No. And even if I...all right, let's say I am. It's not like education matters to you. The only reason you're even here is the free medical insurance. If

Michael gets in, you'll still be making snide remarks, and Ethan's life will be ruined, all because of you.

(As ALLIE *exits)*

GWEN: How can you be so selfish?! *(She returns to* CLAIRE*'s office)* All right…"A", I never tried to call him, / "B"…

CLAIRE: Sit down, please.

GWEN: Was this morning all just to punish me? "Let's get Gwen excited / by telling her…"

CLAIRE: You made contact with a donor. You jeopardized *five years* worth of…sit!

*(*GWEN *sits.)*

CLAIRE: Apparently this isn't the first time you've been dishonest with us.

GWEN: What do you / mean?

CLAIRE: If I hadn't called your old committee chairman, I'd never have known about your orals.

GWEN: "My…"? I didn't pass them. I've never tried to hide that.

CLAIRE: What about how you couldn't breathe and ran out of the room?

GWEN: Since when does every little personal detail / have to…?

CLAIRE: "Little"? Campus security became involved. You told your roommate you wanted to jump off a bridge.

GWEN: I didn't mean it.

CLAIRE: Obviously, although you really need to stop saying it to people.

GWEN: Ethan never did anything wrong…please don't punish him because of me.

CLAIRE: *(Beat)* How long have you been sending C2 recordings?

GWEN: Less than a year.

CLAIRE: Does that mean the same thing as *almost* a year?

(Slight beat, then GWEN nods yes.)

CLAIRE: Thank you. Maybe you can explain...

(CLAIRE hands GWEN a bound, professional looking document.)

GWEN: What's this?

CLAIRE: *(Focusing on her own copy of the same pages)* An exact transcript of that recording we found. Here's where you ask C2's advice about buying Ethan a dog... second page, third paragraph, if you want to follow along...

(As CLAIRE continues to flip pages:)

GWEN: Is this really / necessary?

CLAIRE: ...then top of page four...when Ethan gets a shot, should you warn him on the car ride over or let the doctor / explain...

GWEN: What's your point?

CLAIRE: This transcript is eight pages long.

GWEN: I wasn't trying to be concise.

CLAIRE: Right now I can afford to be flip...you can't. *(Slight beat, as she turns back to the transcript)*

GWEN: I knew he couldn't answer. Just having him listen was enough.

CLAIRE: Okay, *here's* where I start to lose you. *(Reading from the transcript)* "When I finally saw the platinum catalogue, I was surprised by how much the donors sounded alike...but when I turned to *your* page, I knew right away.'" *(She stops reading.)* Knew what? He'd be the perfect *donor*?

GWEN: I guess.

CLAIRE: Probably a lot of things.

GWEN: Probably.

CLAIRE: Like what? The perfect *father*? *(Slight beat)* Here's the part that really… *(Reading)* "When you think about all the children who believe they were born into the wrong family by accident, isn't it possible that *some* of them are right"'

GWEN: All I meant / by that…

CLAIRE: "Take me and Pete. He got some girl pregnant in college, and I conceived here the first time I tried… so how come I couldn't get pregnant with Pete?"…

(CLAIRE ignores GWEN's obvious desire for a chance to explain.)

CLAIRE: … "There are a million possible reasons, so why couldn't one of them be that Ethan was never meant to be with him?"

GWEN: I can see how that must / have sounded…

CLAIRE: No. I realize a lot of people…you hear them at parties going on about some couple that were clearly meant to be together, because one of them worked in a shoe store, and the other needed shoes, but you're a *scientist.* "The wrong family"…"meant to be with"… *(Pointing to a particular place in her own copy)* Read this part for me.

GWEN: Why?

CLAIRE: From "Whenever someone asked Pete…"

GWEN: *(Slight beat, then complying)* "Whenever someone asked Pete if he felt threatened, using a genius as the donor, he'd say, `Why? That guy's only the donor. I'm the father, and that will never change'." *(She puts down the transcript)*

CLAIRE: Why did you stop?

GWEN: I didn't know you wanted me to / keep...

CLAIRE: Pete says he's the father, that will never change, and then *you* say...

GWEN: *(Slight beat, before anxiously resuming)* "But it did for me. No matter how deeply I looked into Ethan's eyes..."

CLAIRE: *(Slight beat)* Umm?

GWEN: ..."I could never find Pete...only you." All right, when you put all those things together, / I can...

CLAIRE: "Only *you*." He's Ethan's sperm donor! ...An I Q in a catalogue /...

GWEN: Why do you have to make it sound / so...?

CLAIRE: That's right, "You knew". You and twenty-three *other* women who picked him for Alexander... Ricardo...Shaniqua...and if we hadn't shut down his line at twenty-four, I'm sure / there *(would've been)*...

GWEN: Ethan saw him! *(Having never intended to say this, she pushes ahead)* His team was playing soccer, when he saw a man sitting in the stands. The man was watching him and smiling...like he already knew Ethan. When Ethan looked up again later, he was gone.

CLAIRE: Did you notice anyone / sitting *(there yourself)*?

GWEN: No, but I was all the way on / the other...

CLAIRE: Do you believe he saw C2?

GWEN: Ethan wouldn't lie.

CLAIRE: No, but he's a little boy, and if he was *expecting* to see a man / ...?

GWEN: Why would he be expecting / to...?

CLAIRE: He never told you for his birthday he wanted his "real father" to watch him play soccer?

GWEN: Who said that? Did his teacher tell you Ethan said that? *(Momentarily uncertain, then rising to the challenge)* And so what if he did? You don't think it's natural when a boy finds out his real father is someone *any* boy would feel proud / to have...

CLAIRE: He wasn't there, Gwen. He didn't watch Ethan play, and he's never *going* to watch Ethan play...

GWEN: You don't know / that.

CLAIRE: Ethan never saw him, because he wasn't there.

GWEN: Maybe you should ask *Ethan* if you're / so...

CLAIRE: Didn't you tell him if that's what he really wanted, he should tell his father himself...?

GWEN: No, why would I / tell *(him that)*...?

CLAIRE: And once his father heard his voice, you were sure he'd want to come?

GWEN: What I *said* was "your father's busy doing important things all over the world, so he might not be *able* / to come".

CLAIRE: Right, the only problem, Ethan is *five*, when you tell a five-year-old his father *might* come on his birthday, that means he *will*...so if a smiling man happens to look in Ethan's general direction just as Ethan is looking into the stands for his father that day, it means his father loves him so much he dropped everything to come see him play...and if Ethan looks up a *second* time, but this time the man is gone, it means his father was so disappointed, he left without even bothering to wish him a happy... Did you think this through at all?!! The only reason Ethan *thought* he saw him was *you* made him believe that if he told his father how much it would mean / (to him)...

GWEN: *No*, that isn't...All I said was if he wanted to say a few words to his father...about *anything*...and if he didn't want to, that was fine / (too)...

(CLAIRE *interrupts by suddenly reaching her phone and pointing it forcefully at* GWEN, *then begins to plays a downloaded excerpt from the recording with Ethan.*)

GWEN'S VOICE: It's okay, sweetie, you won't be bothering him. He *wants* you to tell him what you'd like for your birthday.

(Inaudible mumbling)

GWEN'S VOICE: Don't be embarrassed, you've got a beautiful voice. Just get a little closer to the microphone and tell your father how much you want him to come see your game. Go on...he needs to hear it from you.

ETHAN'S VOICE: Daddy?

(The word seems to hang in the air forever. seeing GWEN'*s stricken expression,* CLAIRE *finally turns off the phone.*)

CLAIRE: Just so you know, Ethan never told his teacher...or anyone. He's very loyal. We only found out about the recordings two weeks ago, because C2 finally told us.

(CLAIRE *sits back, giving* GWEN *enough time to begin grasping not just that C2 had exposed her but that* CLAIRE *had more than one recording.*)

CLAIRE: The only reason he waited so long was he didn't want to get you in trouble. He said he just assumed if he didn't respond, eventually...but when you *didn't* stop... *(Beat)* I can only imagine how hard it would've been for him to resist coming to see Ethan play, once he heard Ethan's voice...thankfully he never heard it.

GWEN: *(Slight beat)* I don't / (understand)...

CLAIRE: That or any of the other recordings you sent him. Once he started listening to the first one and realized what you were doing, all the others went right into this box.

(Before handing GWEN *the box with the disks,* CLAIRE *rattles it slightly, but* GWEN *seems to be frozen and does not react.* CLAIRE *offers her the box more insistently, until* GWEN *finally takes it, opening it fearfully, as she might a box full of snakes, and stares into it.* CLAIRE *waits for her to look up, but* GWEN *continues to stare.)*

CLAIRE: Gwen? *(A couple of beats)* I don't know if you appreciate how many...Gwen!

*(*GWEN *finally looks up.)*

CLAIRE: A lot of very brilliant, important people have been working around the clock for five years. We realize getting everyone to accept this school won't be easy. There will always be small-minded people who would be happy to see to us all go back to living in a cave. They'll make up stories about the program...say black is white to scare the others...so we'll just have to work that much harder to reassure them the school is a wholesome place...full of laughing children and pleasant, rational soccer moms who aren't running amok, jeopardizing the program, and confusing their children by promising them something they'll never have.

GWEN: *(Beat)* I just thought if his father could hear Ethan's voice...he'd realize Ethan is more than some number between one and twenty-four. He's a real five-year-old boy, and he needs... *(Beat)* I just wanted him to have...

CLAIRE: *(Slight beat)* I know.

GWEN: Do you think he'll ever get over what I did to him?

CLAIRE: *(Slight beat, carefully)* He knows you love him.

(Beat. GWEN *looks into the box one last time, then puts the cover back on and returns the box to* CLAIRE*)*

CLAIRE: I'm sorry I had to do things this way. I wish we could have sat here and discussed this like two scientists trying to solve a technical problem, but I don't think you'd have seen what a mad, impossible idea...and whatever you promised, I wouldn't have believed you. *(Slight beat)* If you think I can't understand...I considered having children once. I had this bright clear picture in my mind of a family. I knew it would take a very particular kind of man to belong in that picture, and when I found him, I thought, "You know, this might actually work". *(Slight beat)* So when I realized it was only a picture, I thought I would die. But I didn't. I survived, and so will you.

GWEN: Yes. Thank you.

CLAIRE: *(Holding up the box of flash memory cards)* So no more of these?

GWEN: I promise.

CLAIRE: *(Slight beat)* I believe you. And in fairness, nothing actually *happened*. C2 never came to watch Ethan play. He never heard Ethan's voice. *(Slight beat)* But that's *not* how people will see it. They'll ask, "How reliable is *any* of our data, when all it took was one mother...?" If those people would only stop and think...but they won't. So it's probably best if this whole thing stays just between us.

GWEN: *(Slight beat, after what seems a flicker of doubt)* Of course. No, you're right.

CLAIRE: Something else your old committee chairman told me. He'd always assumed you would take a leave...deal with your problem...and then sail through your orals the next time. "You had so much promise", he said. Have you ever thought about going back?

GWEN: My entire committee thought I was having a seizure. Campus security showed up at my dorm with tongue depressors.

CLAIRE: I'm sure one phone call from Doctor Vorsiff to your committee…

GWEN: I haven't done any original research in almost… not that it was ever all that original.

CLAIRE: Did you notice the moment I paid you a compliment /…?

GWEN: Originality just isn't my forte, but from the time I was little, I've always had a flair for research design.

CLAIRE: A kind of "innate instinct"…that's what Doctor Vorsiff said about your dissertation.

GWEN: You don't mean he's read it?

CLAIRE: How else could he offer to call?

GWEN: I'm just so…that he would take the time / to (actually)…

CLAIRE: Not all of it, of course, but that's what makes Doctor Vorsiff unique…his ability to grasp the whole from even a sliver. I also thought…as we begin to refine our new student assessment tools…if we had someone who could give us a *parent's* perspective…

(As GWEN *starts to protest)*

CLAIRE: It's not a favor…we'll need a parent who also understands research design. I can't make any promises about Ethan…officially. But if you can make Doctor Vorsiff believe you're the Gwen I'm seeing right now instead of the one who *used* to cause trouble… would that work for you? The Ph.D…sitting in on the meetings…?

GWEN: Well…if Doctor Vorsiff really feels my input…
(Slight beat) I think the problem…Ethan's the only thing
that keeps me grounded, but if I also had work…work
that *matters*…

CLAIRE: Then make it happen. Doctor Vorsiff's waiting
for you.

*(CLAIRE stands and opens the upstage door for the first time,
gesturing for GWEN to follow. As they exit, lights shift to
the waiting room, as ALLIE and TOM enter.)*

ALLIE: Thanks for coming back. I know you felt we
were ganging up / on you.

TOM: Listen, I wanted say this anyway. I was going
over things from this morning, when I had this
amazing insight /…

ALLIE: And I really want to hear / it…

TOM: I half expected to see a bolt of / lightening…

ALLIE: That's great, but first I need to explain / why…

TOM: Admittedly I did have a couple of beers…

ALLIE: Oh.

TOM: Just two…I never even finished the second / one.

ALLIE: No, I / wasn't…

TOM: I didn't want to say anything till the beers wore
off, that's / why…

ALLIE: *Tom.* We're meeting with Doctor Vorsiff at one.

TOM: What for?

ALLIE: *(Taking the pages about the school from her purse)*
There's a brand new school Claire was telling me that
Michael might be able to go, where the other kids are
like him, and all the teachers are specially…can you
imagine, there's an entire course just on telescopes…

TOM: Jesus, it never ends with these people!

ALLIE: All Claire's asking is for us to meet with Vorsiff and listen.

TOM: That's all people ever ask. By the time you get in your car, you own a time share. *(Slight beat)* Public school wasn't good enough…now the place he goes with the ten million dollar swing set isn't either? You ask me, the school Michael's in now is hoity toity enough.

ALLIE: Tom…at Back to School night…did you notice the parking lot? Half the parents drive Suburus like us. They only seem hoity toity, because they didn't drop out of school. *(Slight beat)* I feel inadequate with Michael just like you. I don't want to be one of those mothers who goes around complaining her kid never talks to her instead of asking why he should, when she's got nothing to say.

TOM: You've got all kinds of things to say.

ALLIE: I read Danielle Steele.

TOM: Everyone's got something they do just for fun.

ALLIE: Some people think reading a novel that's <u>decent</u> is fun.

TOM: At least you read, that's / something.

ALLIE: There's a book group less than two blocks at the library, and I've (never even gone)…is any of this getting through to you?

TOM: "There's a book group"…I think that's a / great idea.

ALLIE: "At least I read"? What am I supposed do with that, feel guilty I don't have dyslexia too?

TOM: All I said was you're right about the book / group.

ALLIE: Every other kid in Michael's class has a mother who's qualified to work with grownups.

TOM: So go back and finish. How many credits / do you...?

ALLIE: I don't want to be a dental hygienist.

TOM: Why not? There's a huge demand, and you've got the perfect personality...plus, you won't have to waste all those years becoming a dentist.

ALLIE: I don't *want* to be a dentist. I don't want <u>any</u> job where I'm looking in somebody's mouth.

TOM: Since when?

ALLIE: I don't know...since I was *three*? I only picked it, because I needed a major, and... Why is this news?! And what do you mean I've got the...what's the perfect personality for working on somebody's mouth?

TOM: You meet some total stranger, five minutes later he's telling you his life story.

ALLIE: Not when he's getting a root canal, and his mouth is full of *equipment*, / Tom.

TOM: I don't know what you're asking / me.

ALLIE: I don't *either*. All I know is I'm thirty-three years old, and I'm sick of boring myself to death. *(Beat)* I don't know if this new school is the answer for Michael, but you and I need to be able to have a conversation in a normal tone of voice, where I can say, 'Tom, Michael *is* "exceptional". I don't like that word any better than you, but he has a special gift, and pretending he's just another kid won't change what he needs, which is teachers who aren't afraid of him and kids who don't treat him like he's from Mars. *(Beat)* And it isn't just Michael. I know I agreed that going with a different kind of donor this time was only fair, but I'm sorry, Tom, fair's got nothing to do with this. I mean, why did we come here in the first place? To give Michael a better life. And if we can do the same for his sister, what choice do we have?

TOM: *(Beat)* Fuck. You know what I wish? The kind of people who try to help by recommending places like this would stop and think for a second and then drop dead. *(Slight beat)* I know it takes me longer to figure things out than you, and I'm totally fine with you being smarter, but don't I always...eventually...? Which reminds me, that insight I was saying? Before we meet Vorsiff, I'm gonna call Murph and tell him I want the job.

ALLIE: No, you were right. If you're just gonna hate what / you're doing...

TOM: Listen, this whole "I hate my job"...I think I've been feeling I *should* hate my job, so I can do something else that Michael won't feel embarrassed telling his friends.

ALLIE: Tom...

TOM: Maybe that's part of the thing with you and people's mouths, except I actually *like* what I do.

ALLIE: That's what I always thought. I guess I assumed / you...

TOM: That's the problem...you always assume. Like that I didn't want a donor for Michael, since why should half of him come from you when there's nothing from me, and I didn't, but only at the very (beginning)...and I'm glad I kept my mouth shut, because I never would've guessed there's a gene for someone's laugh, but Michael's got the exact same laugh as you. Hearing you laugh was the first thing I fell in love with, so when the two of you start cracking each other up, it's like hearing my favorite song in stereo.

ALLIE: *(Genuinely touched)* Wow.

TOM: Just because I think you'd make a great dental hygienist doesn't mean I don't know you.

ALLIE: I didn't / mean that.

TOM: Or I can't relate to that whole weird blood sister thing you have with Janet and Beth, and I can…kind of. Even if I'm not all that crazy about Janet…or her voice… *(Slight beat)* Sometimes I miss my brother Frank so much I feel like crying, and I know you think that's a lot weirder, which it easily is. All I have is a picture dad took of him bundled up in front of a snowman a month before he died, but every year on his birthday, you cut fresh flowers and go with me to his grave, and if you knew one-tenth of how much that means…

(Beat)

ALLIE: Michael wet the bed.

TOM: I know, he told me. *(Slight beat)* What, you thought I'd be upset?

ALLIE: No, I'm just surprised you never (mentioned)… what did you say?

TOM: Mostly how when I was his age, I peed on myself a bunch of times, only I was awake. My mind would be into some project, when suddenly something warm…I told him how it always felt "warm" right before it felt "wet"…he thought that was really interesting. Then I said, 'It's probably different for every kid, but the good news is no one's still doing it when he gets to be my age.'

(Lights fade. when they come up again, several hours have passed. Late afternoon. GWEN is alone in the waiting room. ALLIE and TOM enter. ALLIE and GWEN seem surprised and a little guilty when they see each other.)

ALLIE: We just got finished meeting with Vorsiff.

GWEN: Oh. I met with him earlier.

ALLIE: You never know…someone could always drop out.

GWEN: I think that's a very mature way to look at it.

(Slight beat. Their surprise has turned into confusion)

ALLIE: You didn't see Claire, did you?

GWEN: No, and I've been waiting an hour. Sorry, that was insensitive.

(Responding to ALLIE's *puzzled expression)*

GWEN: Complaining about a little inconvenience…I mean, considering the circumstances.

ALLIE: I think this is one time you're completely entitled / to feel…

GWEN: In fact, if you'd like to see her first…my meeting will probably take awhile.

ALLIE: That's okay, so will ours…they always give you a million forms to fill out.

TOM: *(Uncomfortably, to* GWEN*)* Listen, I just want to say…

GWEN: *(Ignoring him)* What forms?

ALLIE: To enroll Michael.

TOM: …I'm sure your kid came really / close…

ALLIE: You don't know? They want to take Michael.

GWEN: No they don't. You must have heard him wrong. They're taking Ethan.

*(*CLAIRE *enters carrying a shopping bag.)*

CLAIRE: Sorry, I tried to squeeze in a little shopping.

GWEN: You're not really taking Michael, are you? She's saying he was accepted too.

CLAIRE: What do you mean "accepted *too*"?

GWEN: You told us they were competing.

CLAIRE: Right, but not against each other.

GWEN: You said both of them were flutes.

TOM: *(Whispering to* ALLIE, *overlapping* CLAIRE'*s response)* "Flutes"?

CLAIRE: Right, but when have you heard an orchestra with only one flute? *(Slight beat)* Let me understand... Did Doctor Vorsiff actually say they've been accepted?

GWEN: He said he was sure Ethan and I would make a wonderful / (contribution)...

CLAIRE: He never mentioned there's one more thing we'll need to discuss?

GWEN: He said something, but it sounded like a formality.

ALLIE: *(As* CLAIRE *turns to her)* He said "a couple of loose ends" to us.

CLAIRE: Interesting.

ALLIE: I just want to say, the school sounds incredible. It was like someone snuck into Michael's brain one night, took a picture of everything that excites him and turned it into a school. Tom loved it too, believe it / or not...

TOM: I make a mistake, I'm the first guy to / admit it.

GWEN: I just wonder if you've really (thought through) ...you know how sensitive Ethan... *(A quick glance at* ALLIE*)* ...and if you're only taking twelve children... I'm not saying Michael...but if, just as an example, one of them tends to be on the loud side, won't / that...?

ALLIE: Did you really / just say...?

CLAIRE: You're right, how the children relate is crucial. That's why we ran each pair through a virtual play assessment. Michael and Ethan were each exceptional in their own right, but together their performance went through the roof, which is why we want...need...both. *(Beat, indicating her office)* Tom...Allie...what if I start with you?

GWEN: Why?

CLAIRE: That's just the order I'm going in.

GWEN: I've been waiting almost an hour. How come she gets to waltz in here / and …?

TOM: *(To* ALLIE*)* I mean, she *was* here first, and if it's that important *(to her)*…?

ALLIE: *(Still focused on* GWEN*)* The only reason you've been waiting is you got to meet with Vorsiff first.

GWEN: Please stop calling him "Vorsiff". It's *Doctor* Vorsiff. He's not your fishing buddy!

CLAIRE: Tom…I need a little time alone with the ladies…you understand. *(Gesturing to* GWEN *and* ALLIE*)* My office?

TOM: *(As the three of them go,* TOM *catches* CLAIRE*)* Can I just…I'm sure you weren't trying to put Michael down, but why did you call him a flute?

(Slight beat)

CLAIRE: Do me a favor and hold onto that question in case I forget to cover it. *(She enters the office, shuts the door and turns to* ALLIE *and* GWEN.*)* Let me be perfectly honest. Everyone on the team agreed that Ethan and Michael deserve to get in, but more than two-thirds wanted to cut them anyway just to avoid dealing with you. *I'm* the reason your sons are still on the list. *(Slight beat)* Any time your boys see you together, you'll be modeling how grownups are *supposed* to behave. There will be zero tolerance for the kind of nonsense I've seen today, so as of right now, unless one of you wants to argue that snippiness is a *good* thing, your children are the children, and you're the adults. *(Slight beat)* Outstanding. Now…why don't you have a seat out there, Gwen, and Allie, you can wait here. I just need to sort out one or / two things…

ALLIE: *(Getting up)* I could wait outside / if you…

CLAIRE: It's no (problem)…*please.*

(ALLIE stops.)

CLAIRE: This'll only take a minute. Sit.

(ALLIE sits. CLAIRE opens the door, and GWEN goes to the waiting room. TOM Begins to stand, expecting CLAIRE to invite him in, but CLAIRE shuts the door. TOM sits down again. After a brief, awkward silence, he notices his bag of donuts on the coffee table. He picks it up and shakes it to get GWEN's attention, then gestures an offer.)

GWEN: No thank you. *(Beat)* I appreciate what you said before.

TOM: You mean who should go first? That was a total miscarriage of justice. *(Slight beat)* Did Doctor Vorsiff get into how he designed the building without any corners? No two walls ever meet at an angle, they just keep curving around. He's hidden every joint.

GWEN: That's because he doesn't believe in rooms. He thinks they send the wrong message, telling children space has a shape.

TOM: Trust me, hiding all those joints isn't easy. And the way he described each step…his attention to detail… *(Slight beat, a sudden wave of feeling)* Sorry… my dad built houses, so construction's a pretty loaded topic for me. *(Slight beat. He offers her the donut bag again)* You sure?

GWEN: I can't eat anything sweet this close to dinner.

TOM: That's the problem with Bavarian Cream, so what if we compromise, and you take the Plain?

GWEN: All right.

(TOM hands it to GWEN, laying a napkin daintily on her lap.)

GWEN: You're a very good salesman.

TOM: You have to be in my line of (work)…how much do you know about calibration devices? In fact, this may be… (*Excitedly pulling out his phone and reading a message*) Yes! Guess who's the new account manager at Murphy and Finn?

GWEN: Congratulations.

TOM: And you heard it first. (*Reading further*) I just need to go in tomorrow for some random test on my urine. I kind of did a complete one eighty from this morning, so he probably wants to make sure it isn't chemical. I'm just gonna… (*Gesturing with his phone that he needs to make a call*)

GWEN: Go ahead. And thank you. (*Then indicating the donut*) This is good.

(*As* TOM *exits, and* GWEN *takes out her journal,* CLAIRE *reenters her office*)

ALLIE: So did you rip him a new one?

CLAIRE: Excuse me?

ALLIE: It sounded like Vorsiff was supposed to tell us something, but then he dumped it on you.

CLAIRE: Doctor Vorsiff's always shied away from telling people things that might upset them. If someone has to have a failing, I can think of plenty that are worse.

ALLIE: Yeah, like making *you* tell them. (*Slight beat*) Hey, none of my business.

CLAIRE: Doctor Vorsiff said you're interested in going back to school. It just so happens… (*Quickly scrolling through her contact list*) …one of our interns is the next town over from you. I'm sure she'd love to watch Michael any / time you…

ALLIE: If we need a sitter, there's a dozen right on our block.

CLAIRE: I just thought you might prefer leaving Michael with a graduate from Barnard who's trained in the model over some teenager who's locked in the bathroom cutting herself.

ALLIE: Is this what you wanted to / discuss?

CLAIRE: No. We need to talk about the boarding requirement.

ALLIE: "Boarding"? You want him to sleep there?

CLAIRE: We're only asking for one night a week with Michael. That's the smallest commitment from *any* child / (we've accepted)...

ALLIE: Why does he have to sleep there at all?

CLAIRE: You know those supple, little girls from Romania who seem to fly around the parallel bars? Their muscles get so tight while they're sleeping, they need to waste hours each day just stretching them out. A child's mind gets just as tight, so we developed a bedtime program to keep it supple *while* he's asleep, and if Michael isn't there / to (work on)...

ALLIE: What if his birthday falls on the same night, and Tom and I want / to take...?

CLAIRE: We're not negotiating, Allie. One night's the best I can do. Most of the children are starting at three or four.

ALLIE: *(Slight beat)* If Tom and I do agree to one night, I don't want to get a phone call from you in six months on how the team just met, and now *two* nights are the best you can do.

CLAIRE: See what happens when Michael's teachers... all his classmates...his entire day...*every* day is the kind of day you would kill for him to have even once.

Six months from now, if anyone's on the phone asking for more nights, it will be you.

ALLIE: *(Beat)* Tom would have to be okay with this.

CLAIRE: Of course…and I think *you* should explain it, since he isn't exactly over the moon about me, while I speak with Gwen.

*(*ALLIE *and* CLAIRE *stand, ready to go to the waiting room.)*

CLAIRE: If she wants to know how many overnights Michael has, don't get into that with her.

ALLIE: You *know* it's the first thing she's going to ask me.

CLAIRE: Just say nothing's been decided.

ALLIE: I won't bring it up, but if she asks me directly…

CLAIRE: Then you say it's up in the air.

ALLIE: I don't think I / can *(do that)*…

CLAIRE: And if she decides not to send Ethan? *(Slight beat)* We can't take Michael without Ethan. As partners, they're our first choice for these two slots, no other children came close, but if either you *or* Gwen says no, we'll have to move on, so if you want to help me help *you*, try not to make a difficult situation any worse. *(She goes to the door.)* Gwen…

GWEN: He had to make a phone call.

CLAIRE: I wanted to speak with you anyway.

GWEN: I thought we were going in order…

CLAIRE: I *did* say that, / but…

GWEN: …First Allie and Tom, then I'll / get to…

CLAIRE: Right, but now we're doing this instead.

*(*GWEN *enters. As* ALLIE *starts to leave,* GWEN *hesitates, then suddenly turns to her.)*

GWEN: I just want to say I'm sorry…for making it sound like I think Michael is probably loud. And for overreacting earlier. Where I work, we all had to drive to some lake and spend a whole day telling each other areas where we could use some improvement. Apparently I do that. Maybe once we get to know each other better…

ALLIE: *(Beat)* Thank you.

CLAIRE: I thought you and I could take a few minutes to go over…

(Slightly impatient, CLAIRE nods to ALLIE, who leaves.)

CLAIRE: …to go over why the team thinks a boarding requirement is crucial if our students / …

GWEN: "Boarding requirement"?

CLAIRE: Obviously, not every night. / He'll be *(able)*…

GWEN: No! Ethan needs his things a certain way at night. Before I can turn off the light, he needs his special cup with some water on the nightstand and his cuddle toys laid out on the bed just so / and…

CLAIRE: We understand how important / …

GWEN: And that's just his *things*. When he's not home…just ask Pete what bedtime was like the last / time (Ethan was there)…

CLAIRE: What's so fascinating, Gwen…after looking at how much time children spend with their mothers, the team discovered that too much can lead to as many problems as too / little.

GWEN: Not in Ethan's (case)…when he was a baby, all he ever / (wanted)…

CLAIRE: I'm sure, but he isn't a baby *now*. Back then he needed all the love you…and he *still* needs it, but only the occasional dollop, not a rich, seven course meal every…*Gwen*.

(GWEN *has suddenly turned and rushed out to the waiting room, followed by* CLAIRE.)

GWEN: *(To* ALLIE*)* Did you know she was going to / tell us…?

CLAIRE: *(Still to* GWEN*)* I'm just trying to explain why / we're…

GWEN: No, Ethan needs me!

CLAIRE: He also needs Vitamin D, but when you give a child too much, his kidneys shut down.

GWEN: *(Beat)* Is that how you see me?

ALLIE: I'm sure Claire didn't mean… *(To* CLAIRE*)* She's his *mother*, you can't say things like / that to…

CLAIRE: This isn't helpful.

(Back to GWEN, *as* ALLIE *struggles to contain herself)*

CLAIRE: It's always hard, Gwen…for *any* of us to see ourselves clearly, and I know you've been trying, but I need you to try even harder right now. When Ethan can't fall asleep at Pete's house, is it really because he misses you, or because any time he starts to relax *anywhere*, he feels he's betraying you.

GWEN: *(Beat)* How often could he come home?

CLAIRE: The team thought weekends…maybe every other weekend to start.

*(*ALLIE *tries not to show how stunned she is.)*

CLAIRE: You can always visit him at the school…attend his recitals and exhibitions. He'll have a block of free time every day before dinner…you could take a walk with him in the orchard. We're counting on you to let him know you miss him, but you're busy, you're content, and it's okay for him have fun.

(Beat)

GWEN: What about Michael? (*Turning to* ALLIE) How many nights does *he* / have to spend?

CLAIRE: I really think it would be more productive to focus on Ethan, don't you?

(*Slight beat, as* GWEN *continues to look at* ALLIE)

CLAIRE: Gwen? Don't you? (*Slight beat*) Gwen?

(GWEN's *initial confidence and determination have begun to weaken, replaced by doubts, fear and finally resignation, as she turns back to* CLAIRE)

GWEN: I guess.

ALLIE: Can I say something? A lot of people when it's their first kid…if you think *she's* tense and controlling, my sister Beth used to call 911 the minute Edie began to sneeze, but after Ray came along, she was like, "Don't drink all the paint, we've still got the fence to do".

CLAIRE: (*Her focus on* GWEN, *after a quick, warning look at* ALLIE) Of course we'll be constantly reviewing, and if Ethan doesn't *need* all those nights…

GWEN: I appreciate / that.

ALLIE: How will you ever know if he's never / (home)…?

GWEN: (*Sharply*) It's all right…thank you. (*Trying to be upbeat, as her tension continues to build*) It's not like I'll be home all day twiddling my thumbs. The way this fall is shaping up…

CLAIRE: I don't think Allie's heard.

GWEN: I'm going to finish my Ph.D.

ALLIE: (*Trying to muster enthusiasm on* GWEN's *behalf*) That's great.

GWEN: And Doctor Vorsiff wants me to be his research associate.

CLAIRE: Plus, Gwen will be starting to date. The reason I went shopping… *(She pulls out a scarf from her bag and gives it to* GWEN*)* I think maybe a little more color from now on?

ALLIE: *(Straining to be more positive)* You know what *would* be cool? If you had another kid, she and my kid could play whenever Ethan and Michael…

GWEN: I don't think so.

ALLIE: …I'm just saying, if your new kid and mine / were…

GWEN: I'd really appreciate if / you didn't…

ALLIE: I'm not saying *tomorrow*…first the guy, right? I just meant, like if you and I wanted to buy them matching outfits and pretend they're / twins…

GWEN: Please stop doing this! *(Unaware that she has crumpled the scarf into a ball)* What makes you think they'd even let me?

ALLIE: Who?

GWEN: *(More to* CLAIRE*)* They know what a terrible mother I am.

ALLIE: You're not a terrible… If I told you every mistake *I've* / made…

GWEN: Then why aren't they taking Michael from you?!

CLAIRE: Nobody said any / thing…

GWEN: Nobody has to. If you told her Michael could only come home…she'd've been out that door so fast… *(Suddenly throwing the balled up scarf down)* I can't go twelve straight days without seeing him…I'll go crazy!

ALLIE: Then tell her no. They can't force / you…

CLAIRE: Allie…

GWEN: No, but they can choose some one else.

ALLIE: They don't *want* someone else…they want Ethan and Michael.

GWEN: What if you're wrong?

ALLIE: *(Conscious of the risk and afraid like* GWEN *but persisting)* Their schools were good enough yesterday. Just pretend today / never…

GWEN: How?! Doctor Vorsiff showed me the kind of future Ethan *could* have. I can't pretend I never saw it, can you? How could I live with myself, if Ethan had to give all that up, because I don't know how to handle… *(To* CLAIRE*)* Please…just another couple of nights…he's all I've got.

CLAIRE: Gwen, I know what I'm asking you to sacrifice, but I honestly believe the life we're offering you instead…

GWEN: I can change. His class has a trip to Washington, I'll tell him I can't be one of the bus moms, but he has to go, and there's no point even trying to talk me out of / …

CLAIRE: This is your nature, Gwen, you can't change who you are. Luckily, evolution has a way of sorting us out and putting us in the perfect niche. When I told you I "considered" having a child with someone once… the truth is, that longing became so intense, I finally had to tell him, and I thought maybe…if only because of how much he hates to upset anyone… so when I saw his reaction…but then we had a long, wonderful talk, and while it took me some time to appreciate, Gwen, that talk kept me from making a huge mistake, because it made me realize I wasn't suited to be a mother. My niche was here.

ALLIE: Your "niche"? That baby would have loved you no matter *what* you were like.

CLAIRE: And I'm sure I would have loved him, no matter what *he* was like, but when I asked myself what would be best for him, I realized...just like you and Tom realized, when you were with Doctor Vorsiff, that choosing a Platinum donor for your next child was the only sensible...and what you really wanted anyway... what *everyone*...because no matter what people *think* they want, deep down they all want a Platinum child. Is that the kind of world we *should* want? Maybe not, Allie...but it's the world your boys will have to live in, so my job...*our* job...is to make sure they're ready for it. *(Slight beat)* You're a mother, and there's nothing you wouldn't do for your child. Nothing. All those other "rebel" thoughts are just something Bob Dylan sang at a rally. But then you already know that. It's why you're here instead of on eBay, trying to find the last batch of "average" semen before it's thrown out. *(Slight beat)* Well...long day. *(Getting a couple of forms from her office)* If the two of you can just sign these, everything else can wait.

(GWEN, looking wrung out and defeated, begins to read the forms. ALLIE doesn't move.)

CLAIRE: All it says is I've explained the terms and conditions. Obviously, until Tom gets here...

(A couple of beats. ALLIE still hasn't moved.)

CLAIRE: Actually, while we're waiting, there's something I'd like both of you to see.

(CLAIRE gets a remote, faces downstage, and clicks it. We hear the rumble of panels sliding apart.)

CLAIRE: I don't usually show these to parents, but sometimes words aren't enough.

(CLAIRE clicks the remote again. We hear muffled voices. ALLIE and GWEN both immediately brighten. They move from their chairs to the love seat for a better view.)

ALLIE: Is that Ethan?

GWEN: Yes. And...?

ALLIE: Yes. How did you get them together?

CLAIRE: They aren't... This is their virtual play assessment. We set up a live feed at each school and... did Ethan and Michael ever mention playing online with children from other schools?

GWEN: Ethan loved those games.

ALLIE: Michael said it was kind of like Skype, only better.

CLAIRE: The system projects whatever they're each doing onto a single screen. Then it scrambles the background and tricks the eye, so it looks like they're in the same room, even to them, and soon they're feeling as if they are.

GWEN: I can't hear a word they're saying. Can you turn up the volume?

CLAIRE: *(Turning it all the way down instead)* First watch without the sound and tell me what you see.

ALLIE: *(A beat, as they stare)* Ethan has incredible focus.

CLAIRE: Doesn't he?

GWEN: I think Michael is focusing nicely too.

CLAIRE: Not really...he needs to work on that...but the thing about Michael... *(She uses the remote to fast forward, then stop)* I'm skipping when he left to get that poster of a maple leaf. Ethan was focusing so hard, he got stuck. Michael is using the leaf as a metaphor. He never attacks a problem with Ethan's intensity, but if you need someone to come at it sideways, Michael's your lad.

ALLIE: *(Beat, staring at the screen)* I'm not sure what just happened, but that was very cool.

CLAIRE: I'm not exactly sure either, even *with* the sound, but things are flowing again. Another boy we took has an I Q of over 250. Microsoft just offered him a job for the summer. He's a contrabassoon. There will always be room in the orchestra for a lonely genius like him, but the problems that lie ahead will be far too complex for any one person ... we'll need great collaborators to solve them. We spent hundreds of hours, every combination of children, and there was only a handful of pitch perfect moments like this one. Neither of your boys ever came close with any other child, but when they were together...I wish you could've been in the room with us, because when it happened a *second* time...I don't think anyone breathed for more than a minute. *(Beat, obviously moved)* I have a few things to do in my office...take your time.

(CLAIRE exits to her office. ALLIE and GWEN continue to watch the screen, sitting side by side.)

ALLIE: They're amazing together, aren't they?

GWEN: I know...their expressions... *(Slight beat)* Ethan's never had a best friend. He's too close to me. Maybe boarding is what he needs.

ALLIE: He's five. How can seeing you every other / weekend...?

GWEN: I don't know...but if I believe in the program, I can't just agree with the parts I like.

ALLIE: Why not?

GWEN: It's intellectually dishonest. Maybe that isn't a problem for you / but...

ALLIE: Gwen.

GWEN: No, you're (right)...I need to work on that.

(ALLIE and GWEN resume watching.)

GWEN: I've never seen Ethan so...what's a good word for it?

ALLIE: Enthralled?

GWEN: *Completely* enthralled.

(Lights dim on ALLIE *and* GWEN *watching, as* CLAIRE *moves downstage, already addressing an audience)*

CLAIRE: Ironically, it's the average woman, not the exceptional one, who will change the world. Instead of continuing to marry the average man she grew up with, she'll eventually realize the child of two average parents doesn't stand a chance. No woman will want to saddle her future child with *two* sets of underperforming genes...not if she's a responsible parent. She'll need to find someone better, and if she can't or doesn't want to bother looking, she can always find him in our catalogue. Meanwhile, her average ex-boyfriend will have to settle for having *his* children with some less than average wife. These two paths will continue to diverge...the "genetic haves", if you will, always evolving...the "have nots" falling further and further behind... *(Slight beat)* Now I don't imagine any of you enjoy seeing other, less fortunate people left behind. Evolution's a powerful train, constantly moving us forward, eyes on the horizon, and I for one wish it could stop at every station. I would like nothing better than to stand here and tell you there's a giant tent stretching all the way across the sky, big enough to cover everyone, but that just wouldn't honest. Evolution can be cruel, I wish it weren't...but it's the only way to get from this imperfect world to a garden full of roses.

*(*CLAIRE *turns to* ALLIE *and* GWEN, *watching them with a tired, satisfied smile like that of a mother watching her children play nicely at the end of a long day.)*

GWEN: I barely recognize Ethan. It's as if he and Michael…and it's all they need. *(Unnoticed by* ALLIE, *she begins to quietly cry.)*

ALLIE: I'm turning up the volume. Did you notice where…Gwen?

(Seeing GWEN, ALLIE *slides closer, allowing* GWEN's *head to rest on her shoulder and gently stroking* GWEN's *hair.)*

GWEN: That feels nice.

ALLIE: I used to cry all the time when my mom died. My sisters would sit with me, let me cry as long as I needed, and stroke my hair.

GWEN: My sister used to put gum in mine. She said she didn't have to be nice, because the hospital made a mistake, and I wasn't really her sister.

ALLIE: This was never our decision. We have to send them…it's where they belong.

*(*ALLIE *and* GWEN *sit in silence for several beats, watching the screen.* TOM *enters.* ALLIE *smiles, giving him an "I'll explain later" look before turning back. As* TOM *looks at the screen, he is clearly struck by something he sees.)*

TOM: What is that, a Sony? The resolution's incredible. *(Slight beat)* I don't know who that other kid, but I don't think I've ever seen Michael…

ALLIE: I know.

(As the light in the room begins to intensify, the volume increases as well. We can now clearly make out the sound of two children laughing, but gradually their laughter is joined by that of other children in an increasingly louder, more complex and disconcerting sound—blending moments of arresting beauty and vitality with others that are darker and more discordant. GWEN, ALLIE *and* TOM *continue to watch and listen, utterly spellbound. lights fade.)*

END OF PLAY